IMPRISONED IN THE BROTHERHOOD

DON C. MARLER

BACKINTYME PUBLISHING
1341 Grapevine Rd
Crofton, KY 42217

SECOND EDITION
© 2015 by Backintyme
ALL RIGHTS RESERVED
Backintyme Publishing
1341 Grapevine Rd.
Crofton, KY 422117
270-985-8568
Website: http://backintyme.biz
Email:backintyme@mehrapublishing.com
Printed in the United States of America
February 2016
ISBN: 978-0-939479-43-6
Library of Congress Control Number: 978-0-939479-10-8
FIRST EDITION
©1973 by Don C. Marler
LIBRARY OF CONGRESS CATALOG CARD NUMBER: 73 -91 09 8
ISBN 0-682-47877-6
Manufactured in the United States of America
Published simultaneously in Canada by Transcanada Books.

Contents

Introduction	ii
Acknowledgments	iv
The Web of Tradition	1
Invitation to Dialogue	11
The Critical Mind	15
The Cloth Curtain	19
Education in the Fundamentalist Church	29
Low Self-Esteem and Grandiosity:	33
Depression: A Universal Disease*	39
Racism: A Mental and Moral Problem	47
Setting the People Free	53
Faith Made Difficult	61
The Case for the Updated Conscience	69
Situation Ethics	77
Conclusion	81
Bibliography	84

Introduction

This book relates issues, thoughts and observations I have struggled with as a Christian and mental health professional. The struggle continues and will continue as one issue leads to another. There are few authorities on the issues identified in this book and I am not one of these few. I am a seeker of truth and meaning for my own life and the assumption is made that this is also true of the reader.

When one moves full tilt into pursuit of truth, he may find that the ground becomes shaky and his resolve to pursue truth wherever she might lead becomes tenuous. One learns that security based upon ignorance, prejudice, illusions, misinformation and blind tradition is a false security indeed. Old guideposts can no longer be relied upon. The prospect of seeking truth and following it fully then is often frightening. Not everyone can face it; some decide to keep their heads in the sand. The illusion of security is more tempting than the fearful journey into the unknown.

Some individuals believe that pursuing truth wherever she leads is dangerous because it destroys or weakens belief and faith. Beliefs should be open to change and one would hope that truth should prevail over mere beliefs. Faith, of course, is different from beliefs and should be strengthened by truth. Does it not require faith to seek truth?

A prerequisite for pursuing truth is the ability to be open and honest with self and the ability to recognize and accept that one doesn't possess all truth. Another is the ability and courage to assume individual responsibility for one's search and for the conclusions one reaches. The alternative to individual interpretation and definition of truth is an institutional definition and interpretation. Since life, religion and spirituality are individual matters, it follows that truth pertaining to them is primarily an individual matter. Therefore, the conclusions, ideas and thoughts expressed in this book are my responsibility.

I grew up in the United Pentecostal Church and am more familiar with it than with other churches. Many of the comments made herein are a result of participation in and observation of that church.

After having lived and worked for most of my life in the South (the so-called Bible Belt) I have concluded that those of fundamentalist belief are more alike than they are different. The book, then, is directed to all fundamentalists specifically and to all Christians generally. The intent of this book is to be challenging, critical and questioning. Although this is a book of various issues and observations, its central theme is that we have imprisoned ourselves and each other in a religious system. The major purpose of this book is to help us see more clearly how this is done. Only after we see this imprisonment clearly can we decide whether we want to keep it this way or to change it. Only then can we decide whether we want to be free or not.

Forty one years have passed since this book was first published.

Don C. Marler
August, 2015

Acknowledgments

The author would like to express appreciation to those persons who read the manuscript and made suggestions. The book is better for those suggestions but the final responsibility for it is mine. Special appreciation is reserved for my wife, Sybil, and son Forrest, who gave up many Sunday afternoons while the book was being written, and to Mrs. Leonna Daniel, who advised, corrected, punctuated and typed faithfully and accurately.

D. C. M.

Dedicated To Sybil and Forrest

The Web of Tradition

A vigorous protesting laity has historically been the strength of Protestantism. The laymen of Martin Luther's time believed in a personal relationship with God and personal responsibility to Him. They rebelled against clericalism (rule by the clergy or rule by ecclesiastical power and policy) and they won freedom for themselves, while Catholics continued under clericalism. In recent times, somehow perhaps by default the Protestant laity has begun to exist in inertia. Clericalism is on the increase in Protestantism and on the decrease in Catholicism. Catholic laymen are exerting increasingly more powerful protest while the Protestant laymen are becoming more accustomed to rule by clerical power. Many Protestant ministers are not comfortable with the situation but are, for reasons which will be discussed later, powerless to change.

Long after Protestantism became established and no longer had much need to protest; Pentecostals became the "dropouts" of the Protestant world and began their own protest movement.

In little over a half century, Pentecostalism has moved from a flaming protest against the traditionalism of the established churches to a tradition bound church where clericalism abounds as in no other Protestant group. The rise of clericalism in Pentecostal churches is parallel to their entanglement with tradition. The church that was once different is now afraid of those who are different; the church that was once critical of tradition is now tradition-bound. The gaping hole torn in the web of tradition by Martin Luther is being repaired by Protestants, especially those of fundamentalist leanings.

The web of tradition is a strong prison and few can escape it. The strength of the web lies in its inherent ability to keep men from assisting each other to freedom. Each man is part of the web and his status among other men is largely determined by how strongly he weaves his corner of the web. The strands of the web are intolerance, fear, prejudice, bigotry, ignorance and labeling.

If a prisoner pulls too vigorously upon the strands, he is ejected or excommunicated—to freedom at last—but with unnecessary pain. He is most secure and advances faster when he repeats the "party line" of his church often and as straight as possible. Often this means that the most harsh, rigid, unloving persons move into positions of leadership.[1] They are predictable and can be depended upon to weave a

---

The author is indebted to Dr. Ron Rea for this observation. He made it in conversation about the leadership of the Church of Christ.

The Web of Tradition

strong web. Curiously, they may want freedom as much as those being led; all are in the web's prison together.

If modern-day Pentecostal ministers are to be taken seriously by their increasingly better-educated and truth-seeking membership, they will at least have to adopt an honest stance. The beginning of such a stance should be open recognition that they don't have all the answers; that they are as all men should be—seekers of truth. The search for truth will have to be a hardnosed search devoid of protecting tradition for tradition's sake. Their job won't be easy.

Pentecostals today are what they are because of and in spite of what early Pentecostal "pioneers" were. These pioneers did many unwise things modem Pentecostals are having to live with today; they projected an image that will be difficult to change. They flaunted ignorance and invited persecution; they blamed God and the devil for things they may have had nothing to do with; they created a "clothesline morality"; they created an atmosphere of anti-intellectualism; they became the "dropouts" from the world of ideas and they set their faces against change, We must decide whether we want to acknowledge their error, as well as their soundness, and then move on to new maturity and new truths or whether we want to defensively, sentimentally and blindly hold on to their tradition regardless of its merit. Our forefathers in religion brought to us some essential truth which cannot be lost or overlooked. These truths are nevertheless embedded in much hypocrisy and many distorted values.

We should apply Ockham's razor to our now formalized and tradition-bound religion. We must preserve the true and pare down the false. After paring down the excess of tradition and ritual, we would then have to return to a personal religion for which we alone are individually responsible. We must, however, bear some responsibility for dealing with the results of the behavior of our forefathers. This is also true regarding the social, political and economic tradition handed down by our forefathers. We will for decades to come have to assume responsibility for the remains of the slave society they created and which many fundamentalists (especially Pentecostals) today identify with positively, Some fundamentalists are confused today because sometimes pulling on an old reliable strand of the web, racial prejudice, causes the entire web to shake.

To be taken seriously, Pentecostal ministers will have to drop the old traditional suspicion and fear of education and the formally educated and prepare themselves for positions of leadership. Many members are standing in a vacuum waiting for leadership. Leadership means leading to new ground; no leadership is needed on familiar grounds. Being

The Web of Tradition

tethered to tradition, we mill around in a circle. There is a significantly large number of Pentecostals and other fundamentalists who no longer believe their ship is going to sail over a precipice; but their ship needs a fearless captain. Few quality leaders are likely to arise in the ministry until the entrance requirements are raised. Pentecostals are curiously inconsistent about what they want in a leader. A short time ago they rejected medical care in favor of direct healing from God—except that they accepted dental care and eye care. Now, they would be outraged if a non-trained man performed any medical practice on them. In care of the physical they want an educated man, but in spiritual matters an educated man is suspect. The day may be near, however, when the demand will be greater for the spiritual leader to prepare himself and to demonstrate a reasonable competence for his work.

When a member of the brotherhood of believers continues shaking the strands of the web and all other measures to stop have failed, we resort to name calling. He's a "nigger lover" if he is not consume by racial hatred, a communist if he supports civil rights, a backslider if he doesn't agree with the party line on clothesline morality (morality equals modest dress to most Pentecostals) or if he doesn't believe in dozens of trivial matters which have become traditional idols. He is liberal (a dirty word to a prisoner of tradition) if he questions certain discrepancies in the Bible. If he doesn't agree with the minister, he is a trouble maker, rebellious or is said to be out of the will of God. After this barrage of name-calling, the prisoner usually stops shaking the prison and consequently no one escapes. The web becomes stronger as a result of this successful tactic.

Perhaps from fear of shaking the strands of the web too hard or for selfish reasons, many ministers are afraid to admit the weakness of the New Testament justification for tithe. The same is true regarding the overemphasis on church attendance. Salvation may be the free gift of God through faith and not works but in the self-made prison of the brotherhood one doesn't go to heaven unless he pays tithe and goes to church at least three times a week. They overlook the statement of Jesus (John 4:21 and 23) that "... the hour cometh, when ye shall neither in this mountain, nor yet at Jerusalem, worship the Father but the hour cometh, and now is, when the true worshippers shall worship the Father in spirit and in truth . ." This notion tends to put the responsibility back on the individual and to take the focus off the religious organization; it is the individual that becomes the sacred temple of God and not the church. For some the church is a good place to hide from God. Not that He is not there but if they are there, they may avoid being alone with Him. Church

The Web of Tradition

attendance and faithful support of its programs tend to become the important thing. The Chinese have a story about a man who went to look for his ox; finding it he rode it home. This was very convenient, but it worked only if he could avoid becoming so attached to the ox that he had to bring it in the house with him. "Shaking the strands of the web and all other measures to stop him." Church attendance is no doubt necessary and helpful but as an end in itself it is a burden; it should be used only as is necessary to get us where we are going.

As Watts[2] suggests, the desire to slip back to an infantile state where one is protected and cared for may account for why many Christians seek mother and father in God and church. He believes that true religion is difficult to achieve until this conflict has been recognized. Of course, not all Christians ask Cod and the church to assume responsibility for them; some try to use God and the church to strengthen their efforts to be responsible for their own behavior. This approach threatens many church members and many ministers. If the minister can keep people dependent upon him, he feels secure.

'Freedom can be an awesome prospect to those who have been for generations imprisoned in the

---

[2] Alan Watts, The Meaning of Happiness (New York: Harper and Row, 1940), p. 98.

brotherhood. They may not know how to assume the responsibility that goes with freedom. To obtain freedom, one has to shake off the shackles of the village mind; he has to look critically at his traditions and he has to be somewhat impervious to the efforts of his brothers to keep him within the bounds of tradition. He has to be secure enough to allow his views to be challenged; he has to allow and encourage disagreement, controversy and criticism. When one reaches the point where he can help a brother to freedom by encouraging him when he shakes the web, then he has himself moved toward freedom. The free man is on his own. He knows that no one and no institution can assume responsibility for him. The road of the free man is lonely and made lonelier by so few traveling with him. Responsibility cannot be avoided by taking refuge behind the doctrines of original sin or predestination; it cannot be avoided by volunteering to remain in prison. Each individual is at least partly responsible for what he is as well as what he is becoming. He can only be imprisoned if he allows himself to be imprisoned. Spirituality is an individual matter which each individual is responsible for developing. Religion and spirituality often exist quite apart from each other, and spirituality is often hindered by organized religion. One of the main hindrances is that organized religion gives its own institutionalized definition of spirituality which supersedes and often outlaws

The Web of Tradition

individual definitions. The institutional definition most often comes down hard on the side of ritualistic and outward manifestations. Spirituality is a many-splendored thing that ought not be regimented, categorized and supervised by the keepers of the prison of the brotherhood.

Is it honorable to make decisions based upon fear of what others think of us? There ought to be better bases for responsible decision-making, It is easy to keep the person who is so afraid in the prison of the brotherhood. If he were to shake the prison's web, it would likely be by accident, and the merest glance from a "true believer" (a keeper of the tradition) would immediately "correct" the situation. Freedom, then, has its price; it takes its toll in the demands of responsibility and not all can bear it. The prison has its rewards: the illusion of security and shelter from responsibility. We have to decide whether or not we want to be free and responsible. As the memorable poet and philosopher Gibran so ably put it, "Judge for yourselves whether you belong with the Slaves of Yesterday or the Free Man of Tomorrow."[3]

---

[2] Khalil Gibran, The Voice of the Master (New York: Citadel Press 1958), p.37.

Invitation to Dialogue

It is no secret that Pentecostals and many other fundamentalists have maintained a non-intellectual, non-educational stance; only experience had positive meaning to them. Perhaps this stance was necessary as a corrective to the heavy emphasis historical churches have placed upon intellectual knowledge about God. Neither the extreme of experience nor the extreme of intellectualism is a healthy balance for Christians. Fundamentalists, like everyone else, are becoming better educated and are beginning to bring their intellect to bear on their experiences. They stand to profit from this venture.

If Christians of the historically more intellectually-oriented churches do not reckon with the value of experience in religion, they will be the losers. Christians of the historical churches have been deprived spiritually because of a lack of meaningful experiences with God while Pentecostals and other fundamentalists have suffered from a lack of intellectual stimulation. Christians of historical churches have ensconced themselves in a shell of intellectualism, and Pentecostals have protected themselves with a holier-than-thou facade. In short, the typical member of the traditional churches is "emotionally hardened" and the typical member of Pentecostal belief, for example, is "intellectually soft." There is evidence that both groups are changing.

Many members of traditional churches are looking for experience to add meaning to their intellectualization about God. There is a growing number of Pentecostals seeking more intellectual involvement in issues relevant to life, religion, morality, values and ethics. Some are willing to remove the holier-than-thou fence that has always protected them from involvement with the real world and from frightening differences seen in people of different races, religions and cultural backgrounds. They look forward to a day when their literature will reflect a dialogue about issues; dialogue which respects the right of others to their own opinions; dialogue that eschews personal attack; dialogue that allows departure from a party line.

Dialogue that engages relevant issues at the emotional and intellectual level will no doubt strain the system, but if we are to be healthy, committed and relevant; and if we hope to attract the young of the future, it must come. The dialogue will be more meaningful if it is opened to laity and clergy alike.

It is fashionable today to speak of the various "gaps" existing between various elements of our society. The gaps between laity and clergy are many: reality, piety, communications and often a credibility

Invitation to Dialogue

gap. The dialogue between laity and clergy could be a powerful force in bridging these gaps and removing the fences with which each has surrounded himself.

The time for confrontation through dialogue is now, before we perish from intellectual starvation. The dialogue can occur in literature of Pentecostal and other fundamentalist churches as journal editors, their boards and writers are able to break down their defenses; it can occur in churches as small group discussion is encouraged by pastors who have removed their own barriers; it can occur between individuals who can reveal themselves to each other. Sunday school classes and Bible study groups offer excellent opportunities for dialogue but it cannot occur if the pastor feels threatened or if the members are overly concerned with how others see them.

Being overly concerned with whether our feelings and ideas are acceptable to others is a liability. This concern often causes us to accept passively whatever is laid before us; it causes us to present our public selves while hiding our real selves our real feelings and ideas. The result is that often we begin to lose contact with our real feelings and have few ideas we can recognize as our own we become alienated. Revealing one's real self is often a most painful process requiring much courage and strength. Dialogue is one method of providing opportunity for coming together in a meaningful sharing of ideas and

Imprisoned in the Brotherhood

feelings. It is only as we share our real feelings and ideas with each other that we can know and love one another as human beings.

Let us burst forth with dialogue ringing with honesty, openness, love, and creativity, Looking forward to greater integration of feeling, experience and thought thus becoming whole persons we can then break down our own protective fences and face each other as real blood and guts people. With the fence gone, we can learn to listen. We can learn compassion, tolerance, for-giveness, pain, sadness, joy and love. These are the burdens and the exuberance of the involved and committed life; let them come.

The Critical Mind

Perhaps the most appealing thing about democracy is that it allows, and, on occasion, encourages criticism. At its worst, democracy ignores the critic and the one with a different idea or a different view; but when the different or opposing idea is repressed, democracy no longer exists. When an organization or government is protected from the criticism or censorship of its public or membership, it loses touch with the needs of that public. The strength of democracy, then, is in the right of citizens to differ and criticize their leaders. The right and ability to be critical is essential to freedom from imprisonment in the brotherhood.

Although church organizations possibly cannot exist as an absolute democracy, a high degree of democracy would be an indication of health, if not strength. On the surface, increasing democracy may sound easy to achieve but it would involve profound change in the present structure of most fundamentalist churches. To achieve it, churches would, at a minimum, have to rethink traditional values, admit to mistakes, allow questioning of absolutes and allow criticism of internal structure, procedures and emphases. The autocratic and dictator methods of leadership are both in some ways easier to achieve than democracy at least in the short run. The democratic process is not as tidy as the dictatorial, for example, but it is more lasting and yields better quality. Therefore, the democratic system may be easier on the minister in the long run. If the minister's goal is to produce conformity and unquestioning acceptance, then any system is better than democracy. If the goal is to produce an efficient system of thought or behavior control, criticism and individual differences must be eliminated. If the goal is to resist change, new ideas must be repressed.

The development of responsibly critical minds is a must in a healthy organization. Fear of criticism and the ferment it can cause reflects doubts about one's position and one's ability to handle the ferment. The critical mind is a threat to custom, tradition and the status quo. The more insecure one is about his tradition or belief, the more critical and repressive one is toward the critic.

There is strength in unity as illustrated in the old story of a father who gave each of his seven sons a stick with a request that each break his stick. After each had broken his stick, the father gave them a bundle of seven sticks, asking each son in turn to break all seven together. Of course, they could not break all of them together. The implication being that if they stayed together as a family, they could not be broken. Could there not also be a different kind of

The Critical Mind

strength in multiplicity or individuality? Multiplicity may produce a different kind of unity or it may be necessary to maintaining unity. Multiplicity is often the lifeblood of an organization, and acquiescence (which is often confused with unity) may be a state of ill health. The superiority of man over animals is revealed in his multiplicity multiplicity of ideas, tastes, desires, etc. A pair of horses perfectly matched for size, intelligence and color is a thing of beauty, whereas a group of people so matched would be frightening.

That necessity is the mother of invention is no doubt true in invention of gadgets, but in the area of creative ideas, dissatisfaction and disagreement may well be the counterpart to necessity. What better expression of God can there be than creative ideas? In creating us in His image, did God not intend us to be creators like Him?

The Cloth Curtain

There is remarkably little difference in the roles of Protestant ministers from group to group, from decade to decade and from person to person. There is remarkably little creative use of church resources for the benefit of the communities they serve. The role of the minister, like the use of church resources, is defined largely by tradition. Church members cannot hear what the minister has to say because of what they want and expect him to say. If he doesn't say what they want to hear; if he doesn't say the traditional things, the members are upset and frightened. The minister who wants to define his role in a way that is different from the traditional definition finds that the bonds of tradition are made fast by his members. They are also reinforced by fellow ministers who may be threatened by change. Thus ministers and church members alike contribute to the imprisonment of each other. Since change is frightening anyway and there is so little support for it, only the strongest can accomplish an individually creative role.

A fresh role definition is difficult to accomplish in a system that teaches implicitly and explicitly that change is bad and that does not comprehend that change based upon pressure may be compromise, but that change based upon new knowledge may be wisdom.

Often unconscious emotional needs help shape the minister's role. One's motive for entry into the ministry is most important. And, until better screening of those entering the ministry is accomplished, church members will continue to suffer at the hands of the incompetent. A man entering the ministry because of an overwhelming sense of personal guilt or low self-esteem or because of needing help in controlling his own anger and aggression cannot be expected to be a competent minister. Kierkegaard came down perhaps too hard on those who are concerned more with themselves than with those being served. "When the religious man talks, it is only a monologue. Being concerned solely about himself, he talks aloud that is what preaching is. If there is somebody listening, he knows nothing of his relationship to this man, except this, that he owes him nothing, for what he has to accomplish is to save himself."[4]

On the other hand, when the minister attempts to deny his own humanity and his human needs and limitations, he becomes alienated from himself. When he tries to be the perfect example (God's man to all

---

[3] Carl Michalson, *The Witness of Kierkegard* (New York: Association Press, 1960), p. 109.

The Cloth Curtain

people in all things), he loses touch with the human attributes of himself and of his members. This is a crucial time in his ongoing definition of his role. If he isn't careful, he will have a wide gap between his public self and private self. All of us have some hiatus between these two selves but when it becomes too great, the private self becomes alienated—we lose touch with it. This losing touch with the private self is a problem with all professions.

People are turned off by the "ministerial manner" (the tone of voice and other mannerisms) that result from the constant presentation of the public self to the exclusion of the private self. They recognize the manner as a cloak—a cloth curtain—behind which the minister is hiding. The manner protects him from exposure to other humans; it protects the minister from seeing and being seen. The curtain hides his feelings, his own fears and hurting, his doubts and desires. It may hide his lack of faith in the people to change and grow, to tolerate uncertainty, doubts and fears. And, as he hides, his effectiveness as a minister is reduced. His hiding (a useless accomplishment) is achieved at great expense to his own mental and emotional health. It is no positive accomplishment to become unselfish by losing the self. The curiosity is that almost everyone recognizes the cloth curtain, but few talk of it. Almost everyone (including the minister) understands that he is "playing a role" as opposed to relating openly and honestly to other human beings. And church members "play" their roles also. They relate to the minister's role not to him as a person; he is the pastor not a human struggling to make the next car payment or to keep two church members from fighting. He relates to the members as "the members the people" not to John and Margret who are in a crisis of doubt or who have their own bills to pay. We are too busy playing roles to see and be seen.

Some ministers seem to be motivated by a desire to make people over in their own image. Those members who are different or obviously imperfect seem, in the eyes of some ministers, to cast a negative reflection on the minister. Acceptance of individual differences by the minister is a great honor to bestow upon the members. Allowing them to grow in different directions and to encourage their differences may be the minister's greatest expression of faith in God's judgment in making every man different in the first place.

We will have come a long way when the minister and the church members can begin to define the role of the minister along lines of his being a liberator rather than a moral policeman, despite the dire warnings of the extreme, repressive traditionalists, modern man is not spiritually bankrupt. Spirituality lies within him like the bud of a flower waiting for

The Cloth Curtain

the proper conditions to bloom. Creativity and spirituality are greatly hindered by the repressive hand of the moral policeman who doesn't realize what the conditions are under which these attributes thrive. We are handicapped from the beginning when our behavior is determined more by trying to avoid doing wrong than by trying to do that which is right, creative or spiritual. The mistake is not in trying to avoid wrong, but in putting emphasis on the negative rather than on the positive. The minister has a greater opportunity than any other professional person in helping release the creative potential in people. If his goal and motive is to be an enabler, liberator, a leader; if he can muster faith in people; if he can accept limitations of himself and the people and if he can accept the differences that creative individuality brings, then the reward of watching the development of people will be sufficient. He can never achieve this goal as long as spirituality is seen as separate from life; not as long as the definition of spirituality is narrow and limiting; not as long as worship and spirituality are viewed as capable of achievement primarily in church under certain conditions which are divorced from one's job, family and community. It cannot be achieved under the philosophy that the proper condition of mankind is spiritual suffering (whatever that is) and/or physical suffering achieved by suppressing or limiting the development of the senses, nor can it be achieved under the philosophy that pleasure is bad or sinful and that work is virtuous. And, it cannot be achieved under the philosophy that the individual should abnegate his own responsibility for determining what is right in favor of letting the minister or church take responsibility for the decision. Only that which is personal can become spiritual, and the minister can only encourage its development; he cannot command its appearance in others. His task is not an easy one and it is likely that he can be successful in helping others develop only if he has been successful in developing his own spirituality. If he has not learned to live a full, meaningful, creative life of freedom, he will have difficulty leading others to that kind of life. If he doesn't see that kind of life as whole-some or desirable, then, of course, any growth will be despite him. The minister who has never experienced a sense of oneness in sexual union with his wife may have difficulty counseling a married couple who have a troubled marriage. And, of course, if he views sex as evil and dangerous, he will probably do harm in his counseling efforts. Considering the enormous opportunity and the extremely difficult role of the minister, it is a disservice to him for religious organizations to grant him ministerial license without his having proper preparation. It is somewhat like sending a soldier to battle without basic training or perhaps more like giving an untrained man a license to practice medicine and the stake may be higher.

The Cloth Curtain

Under these conditions, the chance of everyone losing is multiplied, Perhaps the minister loses as much as anyone for he is placed in a profession from which it is most difficult to escape and anything he accomplishes will likely be at an unnecessarily great expense of energy to him.

Education in the Fundamentalist Church

Good education may be the best vehicle for liberating the imprisoned. Many fundamentalists are doubtful of their own beliefs, and, having little self-confidence, doubt their ability to successfully receive formal education. In short, they are suspicious of formal education and the formally educated.

The so-called Bible colleges are now getting large and numerous enough to be greatly influential. We are giving time, effort and money to the various colleges and it would seem wise to ask why we are giving to these schools. What do we expect of the schools? What are we getting from them?

Since the constitution or bylaws of the schools have usually not been made public, we do not know their primary purpose. We assume that the primary purpose of each of the schools is education of students and those secondary purposes may include spiritual, cultural or personal development. There are many indications that one of the secondary purposes spiritual development (with a narrow definition of "spiritual") is being made the primary purpose in many of these colleges. Since spirituality cannot be separated from the totality of life, specific focus on it creates an artificial situation.

Saying that educational and intellectual development rather than spiritual development should be the primary purpose of our schools may sound like heresy but it should be said anyway. There is no implication here that spirituality should be secondary in the lives of the students; indeed, it should pervade all aspects of life. Spiritual development of the student should be the primary purpose of the pastor, the church and the home. The student should have considerable spiritual development when he leaves the church to go to Bible school. Are the churches asking the schools to do the job of the church as many parents are asking the public grade schools to do their jobs for them as reflected in their demand that religion be included in the state educational plan?

Creating schools that are just elaborated churches is a duplication of effort and as such is a waste of time, effort and money. Statements by school officials and discussions with students of several of these schools indicate that this duplication is occurring Some schools seem more concerned with maintaining a public image of spirituality (again in the narrow sense) than they are in maintaining academic excellence; therefore, students are spending years of time, much effort and money for a second-, third-or fourth-rate education. This is a cruel farce. One should get first-class preparation for the ministry or any kind of Christian work.

Education in the Fundamentalist Church

The neglect of academic excellence in some schools is reflected in the very limited variety of courses offered, the lack of qualified staff and poor library facilities. Some schools do not have anything approaching adequate library facilities,

Among many Pentecostals especially there is an irrational fear and distrust of education and of formally-educated people. There is a widespread idea that education kills spirituality; that it is dangerous and perhaps sinful to be exposed to or to entertain conflicting ideas and doctrines. Academic freedom is viewed with great distrust and alarm. Professors and teachers are seen as beguiling people who will some way lead us into sin and away from our religious beliefs all of which implies that we do not feel secure in our own beliefs. We seem afraid that our ideas and beliefs cannot stand the test of these new ideas. So we stick our heads in the sands of spirituality and emotionalism, refusing to face the vast world of ideas.

We must learn that it is in the world of ideas that man is struggling today and we will have to meet and deal with these ideas if we are to be effective. We are bored because of our sparse intellectual stimulation. Tradition has imprisoned our intellect. We may need spiritual development, and, if we do, the main impetus for it should come from the church and from life; but we definitely need an intellectual uplift and this should come from our schools.

Imprisoned in the Brotherhood

If we want schools to provide a first-rate academic program for student Christian workers, then we should make our desires known and our support a reality. If we do not want academic excellence, we can make of our schools a group of continuous revival meetings where we get an emotional uplift and we remain an island unto ourselves; where we are protected from the dangerous ideas of the world; where the world cannot communicate with us or we with it; where we can feel safe and secure in the shelter of tradition.

A student entering a Bible college ought to understand clearly what advantages and disadvantages there are in such a school as opposed to a secular college. The plan he chooses should be in harmony with his ultimate goals in life. He should evaluate the quality of education he will receive.

It is becoming increasingly clear that many of the Pentecostal membership, for example, are better educated and adjusted to life than are their ministers even those ministers receiving so-called Bible school education. The education gap between members and ministers will become increasingly troublesome as it grows wider. One of our greatest resources is time. The unprepared, incompetent minister is, if not actively destructive, an instrument through which we can waste large amounts of time. We will never get maximum benefit from our time, money and effort

Education in the Fundamentalist Church

until competent, well-prepared ministers are available to us. Alas! The Bible schools are seldom meeting the demand. They are instead often havens for the mediocre, the frightened, the narrow-minded, and the maladjusted. Recruitment and educational performance standards are low. Instead of acting as agents through which one gains freedom, the schools often reinforce the prison bonds. How long will a progressively more enlightened church membership tolerate such mediocrity?

Low Self-Esteem and Grandiosity:

A Modern Day Paradox

Mankind, especially those of us who happen to be modem westernized Christians, seems prone to alternate between the extremes of feeling worthless and all-powerful. We deliberately kill ourselves in unprecedented numbers and we demonstrate we can send a man to the moon and return him to earth. Christianity teaches that man is unworthy; his righteousness is as "filthy rags" in the sight of God and at the same time that he is God's highest creation-created in His own image. In a recent sermon, the minister said, "We are worthless. When we think we are worth something, we should remember we are still human." The same minister speaks often of our being "God's people." Christianity also teaches that Christ's death on the cross was the sacrifice for our sins and that no further sacrifice is needed; yet, sacrifice is still valued today as a mode of life. We have even gone further than the old concept of physical sacrifice; we value spiritual sacrifice. What is spiritual sacrifice and what value is there in it? Could it be that low self-esteem, feelings of worthlessness', need for spiritual sacrifice and sense of guilt are all interrelated?

Imprisoned in the Brotherhood

Pentecostals seem particularly prone to suffer from an acute sense of low self-esteem. We handle these feelings in several ways: we become excessively "humble"; we openly flaunt our poverty, ignorance or other characteristics about which we are uncomfortable; we display the opposite (we become a child of the King) or we are chronically depressed; we claim to have a burden (responsibility) for the world a most grandiose idea. Perhaps it is as Hoffer[5] suggests: self-hatred endows one with exceptional facility for united action. When one hates the self, he often seeks a compact group. The feeling of low self-esteem or worthlessness is often covered up by a holier-than-thou attitude. Can we bear to be less holy? Could we accept ourselves if we admit we are not altogether holy? Is the question better stated not as can God accept us but can we accept ourselves? If we are to love our neighbors as ourselves, we should be certain that we love ourselves first some persons move back and forth between these reactions with amazing rapidity. Many feel that the only way they will be acceptable to God is to get continual forgiveness, to make continual or frequent sacrifice, to continually repent or to be continually in prayer. Their humanity (they say) is of no value it is a negative which should be "overcome" or put into

---

[4] Eric Hoffer, *The Passionate State of Mind* (New York: Harper and Row, 1954), p. 34.

Education in the Fundamentalist Church

subjection. This view of spirituality tends to imprison us and kill spirituality.

The view of man's spirituality being inherent in his natural senses and of spiritual growth being linked with reaching a harmonious relationship between these senses and nature is foreign to most fundamental Christians. To most fundamentalists, sexual union or swimming in the moonlight is sexual union or swimming in the moonlight, nothing else; except that it may be sinful. These activities would hardly ever be viewed as spiritual or in any way connected with spirituality. Too often spirituality is seen as existing only in church worship or in prayer. It is precisely because we are human that we are valuable in God's sight and therefore our humanity should be valued by us. All men must be recognized as having value because they are men not because they are men of a certain color or economic status, have a certain capacity for production or belong to a certain religion.

Mental health experts (especially those psychoanalytically oriented) agree that the basis for self-esteem is laid in the first two or three years of life. An oversimplified explanation of how this comes about is as follows. The infant sees the parents as all-powerful as perfect. They are the givers of love, acceptance and attention. The infant doesn't think of these things in abstract terms but he feels them. He gets his feeling of self-worth from the way he is treated from the quality of the relationship. If the mother is anxious or upset while feeding him (regardless of the reason for her disturbance) the child is likely to feel he caused it therefore he is bad. If the mother is upset because of the child's bowel movement, he will feel again that he is bad in rejecting his feces, she rejects him. If the mother sees him playing with his genitals, she may get anxious and upset further reinforcing the rejection and badness of the child. It should be noted that a few occurrences of parental reactions are not likely to have harmful effects, but repeated or severe instances may well have negative effects, especially if they occur over an extended time.

Everyone wants acceptance and interpersonal security. For those who experienced rejection as infants and in early childhood, the need may be more acute. Lifetimes are often spent seeking reassurance from "parent figures" that one is acceptable. Lacking the inner confidence built on early infantile reassurance, we seek reassurance and acceptance from schoolteachers and later from spouses, bosses, and, yes, from the church (mother) and the minister (father). As mentioned earlier, spirituality and true religion cannot be achieved until we move beyond the consuming need to get mother's reassurance through the church. We are at the stage of no growth. We are,

Education in the Fundamentalist Church

as the mental health experts say, "fixated" at this level and as the youth say, we are "hung up" on over concern with whether we are acceptable to ourselves, to our fellow man, and to God. In short, we are afraid to risk rejection, so we hide and conform.
Preoccupation with the minutiae of holiness is only one example of our hang-up. just as the infant whose feces has been rejected tries to win mother's love by conforming and in extreme cases by becoming excessively clean and neat, we try to win love and acceptance by being "spotless." In this, we deny our humanity and try to cover our limitations. How can one then love one's neighbor who is likely to be quite human and in our eyes less than spotless.

Depression: A Universal Disease

From Adam to the present, mankind has experienced depression. This is perhaps the most universal human condition. It is experienced by the young and the old; rich and poor; successful and the unsuccessful; male and female; believers and nonbelievers. This affliction, resulting in many suicides and much misery, is not, however, totally bad for everyone who experiences it. For some, it is an opportunity for self-evaluation and an opportunity for restoration of life at a realistic down-to-earth level. Cramer' suggests[6] that this is what Jesus had in mind in the second Beatitude: "Blessed are they that mourn, for they shall be comforted." (Matthew 5:4). After having looked at the causes of his mourning (depression), the individual may be stronger than before. For the majority of us most of the time, however, depression is destructive.

Grief is normal emotional reaction to loss—usually loss of easily recognized external objects. Grief may become depression when it is out of proportion to the loss or when it persists an unusually

---

[5] Raymond L. Cramer, *The Psychology of Jesus and Mental Health* (Grand Rapids:Zondervan, 1959), p. 54.

*The Article is used by permission of Don C. Marler *Science and Scripture*, 2, No. 5. (November - December, 1972), pp. 15-16.

long period of time. Depression may be described as morbid sadness, dejection or melancholy. It has many causes and many symptoms. The manifestations of this condition probably vary with different cultural settings and different eras, Depression is often caused by one or a combination of the following: low self-esteem, which is in itself usually caused by rejection and a lack of love in infancy; guilt, which may be real or imagined; loss of a loved one; anger turned upon self; and by the shock resulting from awareness that one is helpless to reach high aspirations one has set for self. (Goals or aspirations may be set unrealistically high because one rejects the self as it is.) It may also be caused by fear of death. Karl Menninger has suggested that some persons mourn their own death in advance.

Generally, depressions may be classified into two types: reactive depression—that which is temporary and which results from current circumstances; psychogenic depression—that which is chronic, usually constituting a way of life. It is the second type which will get attention here.

The chronically or easily depressed person often has a low self-esteem. Simply stated, the young child develops the feeling that he is unloved. He feels he is unloved not because the parents are unable to love, but because he is himself unlovable—not worthy of their love. Out of this feeling may come several

Education in the Fundamentalist Church

patterns of behavior. The individual may grow up seeking love by conforming, polite, over conscientious actions. He may develop a severe attitude toward himself, blaming himself with imagined sins, demanding high performance, setting personal goals unrealistically high, driving himself ruthlessly, and denying himself pleasure or relaxation. He may be severely critical and intolerant of others—attempting to build himself up by tearing them down. He may become ineffective, unproductive, and restless. He may experience loss of sleep, loss of appetite, loss of sexual desire, increase in symptoms of physical illnesses, and may become easily fatigued and irritable. He may destroy himself slowly by drinking, smoking or eating too much or rapidly by the gun or an overdose of pills. All of the above actions are expressions of self-hate. Because of low self-esteem, the person does not like himself and makes it difficult for others to like him even though he wants them to.

Unfortunately, the feelings of low self-esteem and self-hate which begin in childhood in interaction with loved ones are often reinforced in school and church. School personnel often do not value and reward a child for what he is but for how well he conforms to what the teacher and the school system want him to be. He is not taught to assume responsibility for his own behavior but is taught to conform to external rules imposed by the system. He is a good person—a person of worth if he produces as expected.

Those persons who are most influential in his church as he grows up are likely to be those very persons who are themselves self-haters. They find it easy to be harsh, rigid and intolerant with themselves and others. They are likely to view all mankind as they view themselves unworthy, no-good, sinful souls. They push and drive themselves to positions of leadership and control in the church. From this position of leadership and influence they can flagellate themselves and their neighbors. They often use the church as a platform from which they teach self-hate. They impose their depression on church members. Listen to a modern-day minister tell of his cure for depression: "You must turn upon yourself, upbraid yourself, condemn yourself . . ."[7] These persons often do fulfill the commandment to "love thy neighbor as thyself." The difficulty is that they have little love for self. These are usually extremely angry people who turn their anger toward others upon themselves.

As Rubin suggests, "Sustained depression equals sustained self-hate."[8] Many depressed individuals

---

[6] D. Martyn Lloyd Jones, *Spiritual Depression*: Its Causes and Cure (Grand Rapids: Grand Rapids Book Mfg., Inc. 1965), p 21.

[7] Theodore I. Rubin, *The Angry Book* (Toronto: Macmillan,

Education in the Fundamentalist Church

present a public self instead of the real self; they fear rejection of the real self by others. They themselves reject the real self and become alienated from it. Many persons who loathe the real self-flee from it by joining highly cohesive groups; thus they become selfless. They subordinate the self to the group. Hoffer stated it well: "A mass movement, particularly in its active, revivalist phase, appeals not to those intent on bolstering and advancing a cherished self, but to those who crave to be rid of an unwanted self."[9]

Selflessness (the loss of self), the ideal of many, is actually one of the most frightening aspects of modern life. As Hoffer suggests, it implies loss of individuality or dehumanization. Those who lose the self for a cause often bring havoc to society. It is to the self that we are first of all responsible. Self-sacrifice is self-destruction with a halo.

Selfishness has become synonymous with evil or sin. The exact meaning of the term as Rand[10] so clearly puts it is "concern with one's own interests." Not until selfishness has been restored to its legitimate place will we stop haling ourselves and teaching others to be self-haters. When we can

---

1969), p. 39.
[8] Eric Hoffer, *The Believer* (New York: Harper and Row, 1951) p.21.
[9] Ayn Rand, The *True Virtue of Selfishness*, (New York: Signet, 1964) p. vii.

legitimately be concerned with our own self-interests, then we can be concerned with our neighbors' interests. Attempting to meet the neighbors' need with no concern for one's own need doesn't work in the long run.

If one is loved by others, he can learn to love self; he can develop the most important prerequisite for mental health, that of high self-esteem. High self-esteem is a must if depression is to be avoided. As Branden suggests, "In order to deal with reality successfully to pursue and achieve the values which his life requires, man needs self-esteem: he needs to be confident of his efficacy and worth."[11]

Mental health treatment of depressed persons is largely a matter of developing a relationship between therapist and patient that fosters a high self-esteem. Helping the depressed person realize he is of value as a human being that he is lovable is not an easy task when the philosophical base of society, the school, church and home continually reinforce the notion that man is basically bad and unworthy.

Just as the physical body needs food for proper growth and strength, the emotional self needs love from others and self. Without this we will be

---

[10] Nathaniel Branden, "*Mental Health verses Mysticism and Self-Sarific,*" in Rand, *The Virtue of Selfishness*, p. 36.

Education in the Fundamentalist Church

insecure, miserable, depressed individuals. With it we can be comfortable enough to relax and take advantage of the many opportunities for self-advancement and pleasure which are at hand

Racism: A Mental and Moral Problem

Racism is a centuries-old affliction that tends to imprison the racist as well as his victim. The Old and New Testament Jews were infamous for it and Gentiles were not immune. Peter had to be put in a trance before he could be cured of it, and today's Christians are by no means immune. Indeed, segregation seems to be an unwritten law in many churches. Jesus received the brunt of Jewish racial hatred on several occasions. Perhaps the major reason for His rejection by the Jews of His day was His message of universal salvation even for Gentiles. Three examples will suffice to illustrate racism in the early church society; then an attempt will be made to discuss present-day racism.

On one occasion, when Jesus had laid their shortcomings at the feet of the Jewish leaders, they said, ". . . Say we not well that thou art a Samaritan, and hast a devil?" (John 8:48) This was their best answer to the charges he enumerated against them; it served to focus attention away from themselves. They could now look away from their shortcomings toward Jesus' heritage. They looked away from something they could change to something He could not change.

Again, when the Jews heard Jesus tell how God had blessed Gentiles through the prophets, they were filled with wrath. (Luke 4:28) And rose up, and thrust him out of the city, and led him unto the brow of the hill whereon their city was built, that they might cast him down headlong." (Luke 4:29) Perhaps this was an early manifestation of the spirit that causes men to defame the cross (the universal symbol of Christianity) by burning it on the lawn of a member of a minority race or to push that man headlong over a cliff all in the name of religion. Jesus was able to pass through their midst unharmed, but many today are less fortunate.

Finally, the Gentiles staged their own racial protest. The occasion was when the Ephesians were protesting Paul's preaching. The Jews put Alexander up to speak. The Ephesians didn't wait to see whether he was for or against Paul. "But when they knew that he was a Jew, all with one voice about the space of two hours cried out, Great is Diana of the Ephesians . (Acts 19:34) Protest rallies are not so new after all. Here was a New Testament crowd that chanted for two hours.

The long history of racism may make it seem inevitable and permanent, but it does not justify its existence.

Racism is now recognized as a mental health problem, and the mental health aspect is a result of an underlying lack of self-esteem. The basic factor in

Racism: A Mental Moral Problem

racism is projecting our own self-doubts and self-hatred onto others. Evidence of racism is everywhere present and it ranges in degree from the slight negative racial reference from the pulpit to the major plank in the politician's platform.

The presence of opposing ideas in an individual without an accompanying conflict between the two ideas is one of the classical symptoms of mental illness. This symptom is clearly evident in racism. The framers of the Constitution of the United States spoke of all men being created equal, and at the same time continued to support slavery. We nearly worship democracy, but our treatment of Indians, Negroes, Mexican-Americans and other minority peoples belies our words and makes democracy impossible in America. We have wasted our chance to make democracy work. We have wasted our chance to serve as a model for the world. Religious groups preach Christ and continue their racism, making mockery of Christianity. We confuse our children with double standards about race we teach them to sing "Jesus loves the little children, red, yellow, black and white," and they sing this song in totally segregated Sunday schools. We continue racism by our failure to welcome all minority groups into our churches, by holding racial feelings individually, and by open negative racial references.

Imprisoned in the Brotherhood

Projecting one's own thoughts, fears, feelings of inadequacy and inferiority onto others is a symptom of mental disturbance. People who are themselves unsure of their social, economic or political standing are frequently the strongest in their racism. Without a minority group to serve as a scapegoat carrying the thoughts and feelings projected upon them, these insecure people would have to face themselves. Leaders who are themselves racists find in racism a powerful uniting force. The mental mechanism of projection serves political leaders well as it is ready-made for developing party loyalty and casting doubt upon the other party. The same mechanism can be effective in churches and other institutions. Unity is thus based on suspicion and distrust of those who may look, think or act differently. Fear of those who are different because they are different is irrational and it often reveals an underlying insecurity.

We are reaping the fruit of the immoral decision of our forefathers to create slavery. Many are exhibiting today the spirit of the slave owner, and therefore the next generation will reap another harvest of suspicion, tension and hate. Racism is a disease so thoroughly entrenched in society that it will be very difficult to eradicate.

Racism can only be cured by changes in individuals. If change is to occur in the individual, he must first recognize in himself the existence of racism

Racism: A Mental Moral Problem

as a problem and then begin to assume responsibility for his own decision-making and behavior. Of course, change often comes slowly and with much effort; but, if one sets as a goal for himself eradication of racism from his life, he has something positive toward which to work. He can then begin to avoid making negative references about persons that are based on race, skin color or other unchangeable natural differences; he can begin to rid himself of myths about racial differences; he can eliminate racial jokes and stereotyped racial labels and names from his conversation; he can try to bring honesty and harmony to his ideas of Christianity, democracy and humanity. He can begin to see himself as a person of value and then he can begin to see human value in others.

If racism is to be cured, each of us will have to muster the courage to give up tradition, forget past racial teachings and practices and learn to love our neighbor as ourselves. Alas! Not many can do it.

Setting the People Free

Man has long struggled to control his sexual passion. Poets, song writers, novelists, philosophers, ministers, legislators, social scientists, policemen and many others have expended major efforts trying to examine, tame, excite or control man's sexuality. Most of us are at once fascinated and frightened by our sexuality. When we are frightened, we respond in a variety of ways. We may preach or teach that sex is dirty, evil, dangerous, immoral; we pass laws which attempt to regulate even the private sexual relationships between husbands and wives; we abstain or feel guilty when we cannot abstain; we deny that we have sexual feelings at all. When we fear that our control is shaky, we often try to strengthen our control by controlling the dress and behavior of the females in our society. As females become more unattractive, males have to exert less energy in control—or so we seem to think. Preoccupation with the length of the female's dress, for example, is rooted in our fear of losing sexual control.

Fundamentalist Christians are generally long on suppression of sexual expression and short on providing legitimate outlets for such expression. From the standpoint of mental health and adequate control of sexuality, denial is the poorest of all defenses. Many psychological defenses coexist with other defenses to control our impulses; this is not usually the case with denial. Successful denial defines the problem feeling or thought away—leaving no grounds for development of other defenses, preparation or control. How can one deal with a feeling one says does not exist? If he tries to deal with it, he is by that act admitting its existence, and denial no longer is working. When the defense of denial breaks down, it is usually with suddenness. The rush of events following the breakdown of denial is often surprising. For example, the minister and lady parishioner who have for too long had intense sexual feelings for each other but could not admit to themselves such a "terrible thing" may suddenly under certain circumstances find themselves involved sexually. When this happens, both usually say it happened suddenly and irresistibly. The only thing sudden about it was the recognition of what was happening. Openness and honesty with oneself and with one another from the beginning would have given better opportunity for dealing with one's feelings. Imposing superhuman or non-human qualities (e.g., I don't have sexual feelings, I can turn my feelings off, he or she is not my spouse; therefore, I cannot—do not—feel anything sexual—thinking about sex or feeling sexual toward a person other than my spouse is sinful; therefore, I cannot—do not—do it) are ways of denying one's humanity. In addition to

Setting the People Free

causing various personality disturbances, denial and over control often lead to the very behavior one is trying so desperately to avoid. Packard[12] recently revealed results of an international survey which indicated that in the United States, males in Eastern (liberal) colleges were more permissive in their attitudes about sex than males in Southern (conservative) colleges, but Southerners had the highest incidence of premarital coital experience.

Kinsey[13] reported that of those men surveyed who had not completed grade school, 98 percent had engaged in premarital intercourse. For those who did not go beyond high school, the percent dropped to 84, and only 67 percent of those who had gone to college had engaged in premarital sex. It is generally agreed that better educated people have a more open, permissive and tolerant attitude about sex. What is less well known is that this attitude may allow them to develop better control.

Too often Christians seek mental health treatment with complaints that their attitudes about sex are causing their marriages to break up or they are personally unhappy and unsatisfied. Sex is such a taboo subject in some religious groups that adult

---

[11] Vance Packard, The Sexual Wilderness (New York: Pocket Books, 1968), p.149.
[12] Alfred C. Kinsey, et al., Sexual Behavior in the Human Male (Philadelphia: W.B. Saunders Co., 1948), p. 352.

members often cannot say basic sexual words; they often mentally disassociate their sexual organs from themselves or mentally disassociate themselves entirely from the sexual act. They often report that when they are engaged in sex, it is as though it were happening to someone else. These persons rarely participate with joyful giving in sex; they let it happen; they endure it as a duty.

Few experiences are as recreating or as spiritual as soul-shaking sex. It is here in the oneness of physical and emotional unity that human loneliness is momentarily transcended. There are too few people who can achieve it in our society. It is difficult to achieve by those who are raised in churches that are preoccupied with "the evils of sex." These same religious groups often put high value on strong marriages with good sexual adjustment an unrealistic expectation considering that the foundation (healthy sexual attitude) has not been laid.

Preoccupation with dress, hair styles and sexual codes is only a diversion from the important issue: how can we behave toward one another responsibly? Preachers now preach against the braless look, but no doubt they preached against wearing the bra when it was invented just a relatively short time ago.

Sex is not an all-or-nothing act, nor does it begin in the bedroom. Sex is not intercourse alone and it is

Setting the People Free

never limited to one's relationship with one person. Every time two people of the opposite sex meet and interact, some degree of sexual feeling exists. Physical appearance, mannerisms, dress, odors and many other factors contribute to making the feeling more or less intense. Sexuality permeates all of our relationships. Our sense of adequacy and self-worth is largely a sense of sexual adequacy and sexual worth. Our attitudes about sex and our sexuality serve as a model for our attitudes and performance in many other areas of life. The man who functions competently in sex is likely to perform more competently as an employee than his neighbor who experiences sexual problems. The man who sees sex as part of his total life experiences is more likely to perform better in sex than the man who tries to turn sex on as he walks into the bed-room. Efforts to desexualize our daily relationships tend to render us generally impotent.

Sexual behavior can be controlled and over control is not necessary. Control begins with recognition that one has sexual feelings, that these feelings are a natural part of life and that they are not evil. Control based upon recognition is on a more solid foundation than control based upon denial and guilt. Sexual feelings exist whether we recognize this or not If we recognize it, we have a good opportunity to control it; if we don't recognize it, we are likely to be controlled by it.

One's sexuality should be considered a resource to be developed rather than an affliction to be overcome. Rejecting one's sexuality is to reject the self. Never in the history of mankind has the opportunity for developing sexuality into a constructive, loving, creative force been so great. And never has the need for it been so great Too often sex is seen as an aggressive, hostile act, characterized by domination, conquest, control, manipulation and intrigue. Indeed, the model parallels closely the model of relations between nations, between large companies, ministers and church members, and too often, relations between husband and wife.

What would happen to the above-described model for interaction between nations, for example, if we indeed adopted a model for sex that is characterized by mutuality, pleasure, creativeness, tenderness, exhilaration, joy and love? Perhaps the modern-day equivalent for beating swords into ploughshares is substitution of soul-shaking climaxes for the destructive discharge of cannon.

Before we can even begin to move in this direction, sex will have to be viewed as a positive good by that most meaningful institution, the church. Currently, however, churchmen can barely talk about

Setting the People Free

sex; sexual language is strange and taboo to them. Perhaps a more basic deterrent to churchmen assuming leadership in this area is the question of how free should the people be. They may be afraid to let individuals define freedom for them-selves. If sexuality is the powerful model portrayed here, it may serve as the model for acquiring freedom. Perhaps churchmen have always known this at the gut level. If this is true, only the most honest and secure can be expected to take leadership in setting the people free.

Faith Made Difficult

Beauty is beauty only in comparison with that which is ugly. Fast is fast only when compared with slow; sweet is sweet only when compared with sour; joy is joy only when compared with sorrow and faith is faith only when compared with doubt. And all of these things exist in degrees with shades of gray separating and often obscuring the black and the white. If it is true that one cannot experience the fullness of joy until he has experienced sorrow, then it follows that he cannot experience the fullness of faith until he has examined his doubt The brotherhood, however, allows little opportunity for expression and examination of doubt. Doubt is suppressed and hidden, which makes it more effective in imprisoning the human spirit To the fundamentalist, the issue of faith versus doubt is too often a black or white issue; one either has faith or he doesn't In the fundamentalist view, one either believes in a literal translation of every word of the Bible or he believes in none of it—in which case he is not a man of faith. This type of thinking leads to the kind of activity described by Watts[14] wherein scientists search the human body for a soul, scholars analyze the writings of Shakespeare

---

[13] Watts, op. cit., p. 1.

for his genius and theologians analyze each word of the Bible for God.

The very act of examining one's doubt is an act of faith, and avoidance of such an examination is lack of faith or at best lack of courage. Fundamentalists often value the expression of faith above truth. The cry "my country (or church or pastor) right or wrong" is the cry of the man who values blind faith over truth. Loyalty to a church, pastor, the Bible or Christianity is often seen as acceptance without questioning. Questioning is viewed as dis-loyalty. Perhaps this kind of thinking was a major factor in the so-called Holy Wars, the support Catholics and Protestants gave Hitler, countless other atrocities committed in the name of religion and several questionable military involvements of the United States in foreign countries. It may have been a factor in the existence and continuation of slavery in this country and it may contribute to racism today.

One of the difficulties with either/or thinking is that once a rigid belief system is formed, all parts of the system must be maintained at all costs. The cost may be blindness, development of illogical thinking, working very hard to explain and justify differences, or living with conflict. This is precisely what is necessary to maintain belief in the absolute infallibility of the Bible. Many people prefer to believe the New Testament, for example, was

Faith Made Difficult

delivered to early Christians in a neat package untouched by profane hands. Ignored is the fact that decisions about which books to include were being taken for several hundred years by various councils. As pointed out by Bishop Pike,[15] the people who would defend the judgment of these councils in selecting the books for inclusion would no doubt reject other decisions of these same councils. Are we willing to see the councils as infallible in one area but not all? A frequent refrain is that God would not allow books included which He didn't want included; yet, inconsistencies in the Bible are explained as errors in translation. Did the God who was overseer of the decisions on which books to include oversee the translation? Was He not able to prevent errors in translation?

Those persons believing in an infallible (to the letter) Bible have to reconcile the differences in what the four gospels report was written on the cross; they have to reconcile the contradictory instructions God gave Noah about how many pairs of animals to bring into the ark. Was it two or seven pairs? Did Jesus cleanse the temple in the beginning of his ministry as John said or just before His death as Matthew reported it? Is childbirth a curse or is it a curse to be barren?

---

[14] James A. Pike, *If This Be Heresy* (New York: Dell, 1967), p. 48.

If the writer of Psalms 137:9 had known his words were to be counted infallible, he might not have written "Happy shall he be, that taketh and dasheth thy little ones against the stones." And Paul no doubt would have been reluctant to predict such an early return of Christ if he had known his words would be considered infallible almost two thousand years later.

Perhaps the most damage occurs when in addition to being considered infallible; the Bible is also considered scientifically accurate. Those who would use it thus must reconcile the account in the creation story in which light, day and night are created on the first day, and the sun and moon on the fourth day. Are not day and night dependent upon the earth's position with the Sun? The Biblical writers thought the earth was fiat; it possessed corners and a foundation. In order to prolong the day, the earth would have to stand still; yet, Gideon had the sun stand still. This does not mean that darkness was not delayed—only that the action of the sun had no part in it, the earth was thought to be stationary and the sun was thought to move across the firmament The idea of earth turning was completely unknown. Christianity resisted this theory when it was proposed because it was not in harmony with the Bible.

Literal acceptance of the Old Testament has led many today to view God as a jealous, cruel, punitive old man who is looking for an excuse to send people

Faith Made Difficult

to hell. And we are encouraged to be like Him; furthermore, we are created in His image. The idea that this is the way early Jews viewed God and that their view is not relevant to Christianity would cause consternation among fundamentalist people. The Old Testament view of God is more valued by and entrenched in most fundamentalist churches than the idea of a loving Jesus. The kind of love Jesus taught has received scant attention in Christendom. Most Christians prefer the Old Testament letter of the law and an eye for an eye model.

There is no good reason why every particular in the Bible should be infallible. Those who insist that the Bible is infallible and that it must be in harmony with modern-day science will have difficulty. Neither God nor the Bible is reduced by presentations of the Bible as relative and fallible. When the enchantment of historical distance entices us to view the Bible as something it is not, then a disservice is done. The Bible does not have answers to every particular in our lives, and blindly proclaiming that it does is dishonest. Refusal to examine evidence is a reflection of lack of faith in oneself and God; it is evidence of basic uncertainty about oneself.

Belief in an infallible Bible is not essential to faith in God. When the doctrine of infallibility is made the foundation of fundamentalist Christian faith and when there is ample evidence that the Bible is fallible, there is little reason for thinking people to take fundamentalist religion seriously. Those who maintain faith do so, the doctrine of infallibility notwithstanding. This doctrine depersonalizes God; it makes of Him a historical God more concerned with ancient customs and laws than with human beings and situations they find themselves in today.

Early Christians had no New Testament and for hundreds of years (before the invention of the printing press) Christians had only limited access to Bibles. After the invention of the press, their need for an infallible word became so great that in 1870 (only a century ago) the Pope was declared infallible. One of his duties was to interpret an infallible Bible. Of course, throughout Christian history, books and passages have been added to and taken away from the New Testament regularly without raising questions in the minds of the common people about its fallibility.

One of the most positive aspects of fundamental Protestantism and especially of Pentecostals is their emphasis on the here-and now personal relationship between God and man. With this orientation, one would expect the fundamentalists to have a skeptical view of tradition, laws of the land and questionable historical Biblical accounts; one would expect their relationship with their fellow man to be guided by agapec love reinforced by daily communion with and guidance from a here-and-now God. Unhappily, it is

Faith Made Difficult

not so; fundamentalists are often staunch defenders of those in authority in government "right or wrong;" their ranks swell with racists, they hold strongly to tradition and Look to each word of the Bible for daily guidance, considering it a prescription book relevant to all people at all times; many have unofficially proclaimed the minister infallible.

Perhaps the great tragedy is that the fundamentalist does not realize the contradiction in these positions. Is this why his imprisonment in the brotherhood is so easily and securely accomplished? Can such a man be set free?

The Case of the Updated Conscience

The Case for the Updated Conscience*

The conscience of man can be a friendly helpful guide or a misinformed tyrant. Mystery, myth and misinformation have clouded our thinking about this part of human personality. Until recent times there was widespread belief that man was born with a conscience, that it was "God-given." The prevalent idea was that man had innate ability to make moral choices, knowledge of right and wrong was inborn. This belief will not stand under the light of reason, social science or the Bible.

An attempt will be made here to briefly review the process of development of the conscience. Since the positive aspects of conscience are commonly recognized and the negative aspects are not, attention will be given to the latter. The term "conscience" is herein used as loosely synonymous with the psychoanalytic term "superego." It is not a structural part of the human anatomy but rather a complex of attitudes, beliefs and memories of put teachings

The conscience, which comprises the moral functions of personality, is formed by a special kind of learning identification. Through this learning process the values, prohibitions and taboos of parents and other authority figures are internalized. That is, they are taken in by the child and made part of himself. As he identifies with his parents he adopts their attitudes, values and beliefs. Sometime before the child is six years of age be begins to avoid certain acts not just because he fears being caught but because he feels within himself they are wrong. He opposes his own wishes in a manner similar to the opposition he sees in his parents. Thus, if the parents demonstrate a severe or rigid conscience the child will develop a severe conscience. If they treat his wrongdoing harshly, his conscience will usually become harsh and severe. The conscience is also influenced by the intensity with which the unacceptable wishes are felt.[16] The more intensely these wishes are felt, the more rigid and severe the conscience will become. When the child becomes an adult, he is likely to treat his children as he was treated when he was a child even though he may have resented the treatment he received from his parents.

The strength of the conscience may vary from very weak to extremely strong—one extreme is as unhealthy as the other. For illustrative purposes, one may view the conscience as being of basically three types: (1) The putty or water type—it has little critical capacity. (2) The spring steel—it can be flexible but returns to center without breaking. It can, however,

---

[15] Charles Brenner, An Elementary Textbook of Psychoanalysis (New York: International Universities Press, 1955), p. 132.

The Case for the Updated Conscience

resist the forces exerted upon it. (3) The cast iron type or pottery type it resists quite well but if the force is too great it shatters or falls apart. Of course, the spring steel type is ideal.

It is this spring steel type conscience that is often difficult for many Christians to develop especially Christians of fundamental belief. Either/or and black/white thinking tends to develop the cast iron type. The spring steel type may involve negotiation, compromise and relativism all of which make many persons in Western society uncomfortable.

The conscience may also be seen as being like a rock it is there and never changes or like a living tree always growing and changing. This latter view is, of course, the healthier one and yet one that causes Christians such anxiety. Growth usually is accompanied by breaking up of old patterns; it involves a painful tearing down of the old and building anew.

Change and growth are particularly difficult for the insecure person. He finds security in the old and familiar ways regardless of their efficacy. The development of the conscience of many is arrested at an early age by the example of parents who cannot change. Change is forbidden; new information, new learning is ignored. Reason has little chance when the conscience reigns supreme. One hears statements in support of the status quo of the conscience: "God never changes" or "If it was good enough for my parents, it is good enough for me."

Since the conscience is made up largely of things taught us at an early age, it follows logically that it can be wrong. If conscience is tied or related to learning then it is logical that if the teachings given by precept or example were in error, then the conscience is misinformed, Paul said he had lived in good conscience always (Acts 23:1). He apparently meant that his persecution of Christians was done in good conscience. Did his conscience change when he became a Christian? The conscience may be loaded with childhood memories and experiences which are now distorted or were from their inception erroneous. It should be constantly updated by new data collected by the intellect and processed by reason; Denial of the desirability of this updating negates the value of learning and often tends to dichotomize knowledge and behavior. Growth and change in conscience is as essential for good mental, emotional and spiritual health as biological growth is to physical health.

An individual who makes a decision he considers a responsible one but yet one that causes him to violate a principle, a principle that became a part of his conscience early and has never been updated, will nevertheless in many instances feel guilty. This guilt is unjustified but is as real as if it were. This type of

The Case for the Updated Conscience

guilt is quite complicated. It involves grief at having to give up a principle symbolically giving up an internalized part of his parents as well as part of himself; it involves anxiety associated with a feeling that nothing can be trusted that all solid ground is slipping away. It may involve fear of disapproval by parents; it may involve anger over having been betrayed by them after all, they presented an absolute principle which he accepted and which proved to be not absolute. Some feelings of guilt are justified and serve useful purposes but as stated previously we are here dealing with the negative aspects of conscience.

Guilt is the emotional pain and tension resulting from action that contradicts the dictates of the conscience. If we could easily update the conscience, there would be no guilt over principles broken in responsible decision-making and responsible behavior. We have not accepted the value of modifying our principles or changing our values as we get new data. What we have learned is to hold on to old principles at any cost, making them absolute and sacred. We have been taught that it is dangerous and wrong to update the conscience. We have learned to follow rules and to feel guilty if we break them. We hide behind the rules of the conscience and tend to become slaves to them. To venture beyond them is to risk pain and rejection.

Imprisoned in the Brotherhood

Use of the conscience as the main guide is prescribed morality. Solutions are prescribed in advance of the occurrence of the problem and stored in the conscience to be retrieved, as is computer information, when a problem arises. Responsible decision-making must involve gathering new data relevant to the situation and it must involve judgment on the part of the individual. The individual, then, has to assume responsibility for his own decisions; he cannot hide behind the prescription. He cannot afford the luxury of living by decisions made by his elders many years ago. If he makes the wrong decision, he alone is responsible; he can no longer justify his decision by citing the prescription or quoting his elders.

When God told Abraham to kill his son, Abraham was faced with a difficult decision. No doubt he had been taught that it was wrong to kill—especially to kill one's son. Yet, it was Cod who told him to do this forbidden deed. Abraham evaluated the situation and chose to go against tradition; against his conscience and to kill his son. If he had indeed killed Isaac, this should have been occasion for regret but not guilt. He would have had to face his friends with his decision and act. He could not have hidden behind a prescribed answer to his problem. The traditional prescriptions did not fit the problem with which he was faced.

The Case for the Updated Conscience

There is more to responsible decision-making than following archaic rules. We must learn to update the conscience. Updating involves keeping an open mind to many different points of view and to entertain the possibility of many alternatives. It involves acceptance of the reality that in a complex world solutions to problems are not always found in simplistic, prescribed rules. Reason and judgment must be freed from an overly severe, rigid, archaic conscience. When this is accomplished, the occasion for unjustified guilt will be greatly lessened. When guilt is lessened then depression, suicide and unmeasured personal anguish will also lessen. When unrealistic guilt is lessened, the individual will be free to spend his energy in more healthy emotional and spiritual growth.

Situation Ethics

Man's most difficult task is responsible decision-making--¬especially difficult to reach are those ethical and moral decisions involving one's fellow man. The vast complexities of today's society, the tremendous increase in numbers of people, the changed life styles of many, the crowded conditions, world wars, widespread poverty, concentrated wealth, rapid technological changes and rapid changes of virtually all aspects of life make the decisions more difficult."[17] Responsible decision-making is more difficult now than in the past precisely because there are more alternatives now. Even within the lifetime of most adults today, there has been a shift from a few stabilized alternatives to seemingly endless possibilities for decisions affecting our brothers. Today a few people have the courage to seek even more alternatives; they seek to refine the alternatives; they seek more data from which higher levels of alternatives may evolve. The majority, however, shrink from this uncertain ground, preferring to seek shelter behind what was once thought to be universal absolutes.

---

[16] For an up-to-date description of change and its effect, see Alvin Toffler's Future Shock (New York: Bantam Books, 1970).

Imprisoned in the Brotherhood

Most fundamentalist Christians fall into this latter group. They are the modern-day legalists. Like the ancient Israelites, they believe the Bible is a rule book (a book of behavioral prescriptions) that should be obeyed to the letter. Joseph Fletcher, in his controversial and much maligned book Situation Ethics: *The New Morality*,[18] points up that Jesus and Paul tried, but failed, to get across the message that each individual was responsible for his own decisions and his own actions—that they were free from the bondage of the law.

For the legalist, rules, laws or principles cannot be broken even in the interest of the brother. The legalists put institutional decisions, laws of the land, customs, tradition and Biblical prescriptions ahead of individual personal decisions. The main responsibility of the legalist is to find the predetermined rule that seems to fit the case at hand and apply it as rigorously as possible. Matching rules with cases could be done much faster, easier and more accurately by computer than by man. The legalist is safe from criticism since his decision is not his own; he merely fills a prescription written by society, his church or the Bible.

---

[17] This chapter, included here because it is so essential to freedom, relies heavily upon Fletcher's *Situation Ethics: The New Morality* (Philadelphia: Westminster Press, 1966).

Situation Ethics

The situationist, on the other hand, considers the maxims of his community and its heritage in his decision-making, but he is prepared to lay them aside if love seems better served by doing so."[19] For love is the only principle the situationist recognizes as universal and absolute. The principle cannot be better stated than as in Galatians 5:14 "For all the law is fulfilled in one word, even in this; Thou shalt love thy neighbor as thyself?' There are basically three types of love: agape is giving, non-reciprocal, neighbor-regarding; *philia* is friendship love and eras is romantic love. Agapec love is that Christian love which demands that one love his neighbor and this includes one's enemies.[20] It is this unselfish calculating love that forms the basis of situation ethics. If we are to love people and use things rather than the reverse, we will learn to lay aside laws, principles and customs if they collide with doing the most loving thing in the situation; we will have to gather data upon which decisions can be made rationally; we will have to risk being wrong; we will have to risk being criticized by legalists. Perhaps most difficult of all, we will have to learn to calculate the greatest good for the most people."[21]

---

[18] Ibid., p. 26.
[19] Ibid., p. 79.
[20] Ibid., p. 92.

Situation ethics "... calls upon us to keep law in a subservient place, so that only love and reason really count when the chips are down!"[22] Rules, laws, principles and ethical decisions are only meaningful as they relate to people. The universal absolute of the situationist to love God and thy neighbor uses laws when they do not conflict with love. When there is conflict (as there is at times), the situationist abandons the law. Thus, if one has to kill, lie or steal to protect his family, he will do so. Furthermore, he would regret the necessity for such action but would not feel guilty or feel that he had sinned. The commandment "Thou shalt not kill" would be meaningless under such circumstances. In discussion with ministerial students in a Bible college, I once asked what they would do if a man hopelessly trapped in a burning automobile asked them to kill him to spare him a more painful death. As one would expect, the answers were varied. Some students thought they should fill the request but wondered if they would have the courage to do it. Others thought they would not be justified in filling the request. One student slept through the discussion, while one young man came up with a classic dodge. He said, "I would not have killed him because Jesus might have come a moment later and my actions would have not been necessary." He was honest enough to admit he was

---

[21] Ibid., p. 31.

seeking shelter from a hard choice. His answer points up the desperateness with which we often seek to avoid the demands of love.

We find other ways of avoiding the demands of love. Often attention is taken off the major demands by focusing on the trivial things. We make dress, TV, length of hair, and recreational activities our major moral concerns. Thus, we can ignore hunger, poverty, illegal wars, racism, population control, and need for humane abortion laws. If we remain slaves to the law, it will be by our own choice. There is a measure of comfort and safety in having one's decisions made for him; but insofar as we look to institutional decisions for the final decision, we are not free. The apostle Paul spoke strongly in favor of freedom from the law. He told the Galatians (Galatians 5:1), "Stand fast therefore in the liberty wherewith Christ hath made us free, and be not entangled again with the yoke of bondage."

Conclusion

The first responsibility we have is to be aware. We are all (to some extent) decision-makers, and this activity requires awareness. Each of us makes decisions, acts and relates to others in a manner dictated by our awareness of ourselves, the environment and our relationship to it. Our values are determined by our awareness, i.e., by the information we have accumulated, the interpretations we have made of that information and by our life experiences. Since everyone has different degrees of awareness, different life experiences, information and interpretations, there is wide diversity in values and behavior. Changes in behavior, values and attitudes come from expanded awareness, for those who seek to expand their awareness; there is hope for responsible behavior and individual growth. These people are living, or open systems; they have intake (expanded awareness through new information) and output (responsible decisions and growth). They are like a growing tree, taking and giving daily—and always changing. Those persons who resist new knowledge, resist change, resist expanding their awareness are essentially dead or closed systems. They are like the steam kettle taken from the fire; it gradually cools to room temperature and interacts minimally with its environment and changes little over time—it produces little. What it has achieved is stability. Is it desirable that individuals or churches maintain equilibrium in a world filled with racial hatred and political wars?

Individuals who are changing, growing and expanding their awareness cannot be in perfect equilibrium. Change sometimes, but not always, means upheaval. Growth often means giving up the

Conclusion

old for the new, and expanding one's awareness requires leaving the familiar for a journey into the unknown. The decision to expand one's awareness is a major decision and it will not be taken by everyone because some have put greater value on remaining on familiar grounds.

Having read this book, the reader has had many opportunities to expand his awareness to begin to escape from the prison of the brotherhood. The decision to escape is a personal one. The process of escaping may be rapid or slow and tedious. Those who want to escape to expand their awareness will have formulated some questions while reading. The purpose of the book will have been fulfilled if the reader is by now asking questions like these: How free is free? How free do I want to be? Do I want to be more responsible? How can I act responsibly in love? Do I want to become more aware? How can I become more aware? What can one depend upon if not on the old guideposts?

Bibliography

Branden, Nathaniel. *Mental Health verses Mysticism and Self-Sacrifice* in Ayn, Rand's *The Virtue of Selfishness.* New York:. Signet, 1964.

Brenner, Charles. *An Elementary Textbook of Psychoanalysis.* New York: International Universities Press, 1955.

Cramer, Raymond L. "The Psychology of Jesus and Mental Health." 54. Grand Rapids: Zondervan, 1959.

Fletcher, Joseph. *Situation Ethics: The New Morality.* Philadelphia : Westminster Press, 1966.

Gibran. *"The Voice of the Master ."* New York: Citadel Press , 1958.

Hoffer, Eric. "The Passionate State of Mind." 34. New York: Harper and Row, 1954.

—. *The True Believer.* New York: Harper and Row, 1951.

Kinsey, Alfred C., Pomeroy, Wardell B., and Martin, Clyde E. *Sexual Behavior in the Human Male.* Philadelphia: W.B. Saunders Co., , 1948.

Lloyd-Jones, D. Martyn. *Spiritual Depression: It's Cause and Cure.* Grand Rapids: Grand Rapids Book Mfg., Inc, 1965.

Marler, Don C. *The Case for the Updated Conscience, Science and Scripture, No. 1.* Vols. Depression: A Universal Disease, Science and Scripture, 2, No 5 (November-December, 1972). 13 ff., January-Febuary, 1972.

Michalson, Carl. "The Witness of Kierkegaarcl ." 109. New York: Association Press, 1960.

Packard, Vance. *The Sexual Wilderness.* New York: Pocket Books, 1968.

Pike, James A. *If This Be Heresy.* New York: Dell, 1967.

Rubin, Theodore I. *THe Angry Book.* Toronto: Macmillan, 1969.

Scripture, Science and. Nov-Dec 1972: 15-16.

Bibliography

Toffler, Alvin. *Future Shock.* New York: Bantam Books, 1970.

Watts, Alan. "The Meaning of Happiness." 98, 1. New York: Harper and Row, 1940.

www.ingramcontent.com/pod-product-compliance
Lightning Source LLC
LaVergne TN
LVHW021411080426
835508LV00020B/2550